26

DATE DUE			
10-8			
10-15			
11-29			
9-26			
1-17			
10-19			

300529

617.6
ROU

Rourke, Arlene C.

Teeth and braces.

Looking Good

TEETH AND BRACES

by Arlene C. Rourke

Rourke Publications, Inc.
Vero Beach, FL 32964

The author wishes to thank the following people for their help in the preparation of this book:

Eileen Griffin for her work on the illustrations in this book. Ms. Griffin is an artist, illustrator and the owner of a graphic arts company.

Dixie Montgomery, owner and director of a modeling school and agency.

I wish to especially thank **Dr. Frank Campione** for his help and encouragement and professional advice during my research on this book.

Library of Congress Cataloging-in-Publication Data

Rourke, Arlene C., 1944-
   Teeth and braces.

   (Looking good)
   Bibliography: p.
   Includes index.
   Summary: Discusses the function, anatomy, and care of teeth, dental problems, and how orthodontists straighten teeth using braces and other appliances.
   1. Teeth—Care and hygiene—Juvenile literature. 2. Orthodontic appliances—Juvenile literature.
[1. Teeth—Care and hygiene. 2. Orthodontics] I. Series: Rourke, Arlene C., 1944-   . Looking good. II. Title.
RK63.R68   1989   617.6   88-11642
ISBN 0-86625-282-7

CONTENTS

FORMATION OF TEETH 4
  Four Types of Teeth 4
  The Anatomy of a Tooth 7
  Tooth Decay and Gum Disease 9

KEEPING YOUR TEETH CLEAN AND HEALTHY 10
  Flossing 10
  Toothpaste 11
  Brushing 11
  Water Irrigators 14
  Vitamins and Your Teeth 15

VISITING THE DENTIST 16
  X-Rays 17
  Cleaning Your Teeth 18
  Filling a Cavity 18

BRACES AND YOU 20
  What Causes Bad Bite? 21
  What Happens if You Don't Correct Bad Bite? 21
  Seeing an Orthodontist 23
  General Rules for Living with Braces 25

PROBLEMS THAT CAN ARISE 27

BIBLIOGRAPHY 30

INDEX 31

FORMATION OF TEETH

Your teeth are the hardest substances in your body. Teeth serve three major functions:

     1—working with saliva, they break food down into small, easily digested bits

     2—with the help of the tongue, teeth produce a variety of sounds which are used in speech

     3—teeth support the muscles around the mouth and give your face its shape

Human beings have two sets of teeth in their lifetimes. Your first teeth were called **deciduous** (baby, milk, or primary) teeth. These twenty teeth were forming in your jaw even before you were born. At six to nine months of age, a baby's gums start to swell and redden. This is a sign that the first baby teeth are about to show themselves. By the time a child is two years old, all the baby teeth should be in place.

Nature is never satisfied. By the age of six or seven, the roots of the baby teeth start to dissolve causing the teeth to fall out. This clears the way for the second and last set of teeth: the **permanent** (adult) teeth. They number thirty-two. Normally they are in place by the age of twenty-one.

Four Types of Teeth

There are four types of tooth formation: incisor, canine, premolar, and molar. Each tooth is designed to fulfill a specific function.

4

DECIDUOUS TEETH

Upper teeth

Central incisors
Lateral incisors
Canines
First molars
Second molars

Second molars
First molars
Canines
Lateral incisors
Central incisors

Lower teeth

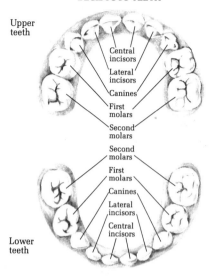

PERMANENT TEETH

Upper teeth

Central incisors
Lateral incisors
Canines
First premolars
Second premolars
First molars
Second molars
Third molars (Wisdom teeth)

Third molars (Wisdom teeth)
Second molars
First molars
Second premolars
First premolars
Canines
Lateral incisors
Central incisors

Lower teeth

6

Incisor teeth are located in the front of the mouth. They are sharp, knife-like teeth because they must bite into food.

Canine comes from the Latin word for "dog." Canines are the four cone shaped teeth next to the incisors. They resemble a dog's fangs, and they are also used to tear off food.

Premolars are also known as "bicuspids." "Bi" means two, and these teeth have two cusps on the biting surface. They are used to crush and grind food.

Molars are the very large teeth in the back of the mouth. They have four cusps. Their mission is to complete the job of grinding so that the food going to the stomach is already ground into fine pieces. The third molars are called "wisdom teeth." Not every adult develops wisdom teeth.

The Anatomy of a Tooth

Each of your teeth is composed of many parts and each part has its own work to do.

The **enamel** is the outer layer of the tooth. It is the hardest tissue in your body. It provides protection for the soft inner parts.

Teeth are composed mostly of **dentin.** Dentin is a yellowish substance located under the enamel. It is softer than enamel but harder than bone.

The **crown** is that part of the tooth which is visible.

A Cross-Section of a Lower Molar Tooth

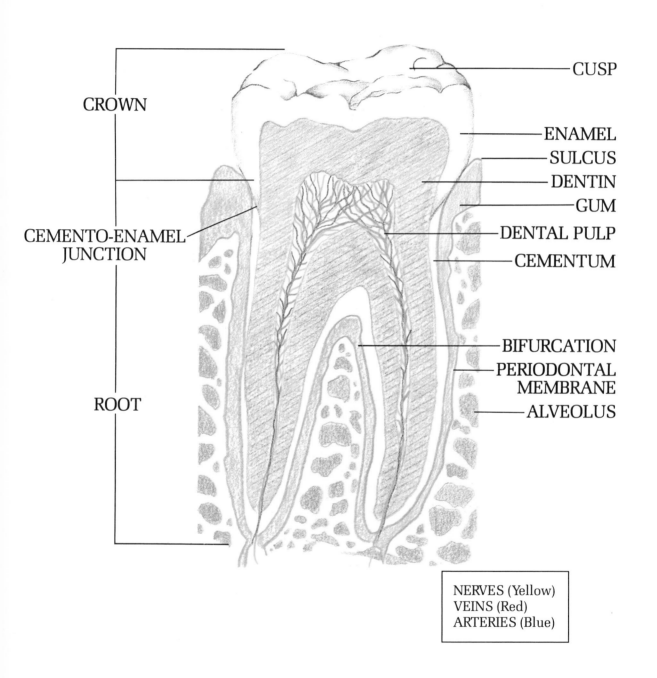

CROWN

CEMENTO-ENAMEL JUNCTION

ROOT

CUSP

ENAMEL

SULCUS

DENTIN

GUM

DENTAL PULP

CEMENTUM

BIFURCATION

PERIODONTAL MEMBRANE

ALVEOLUS

NERVES (Yellow)
VEINS (Red)
ARTERIES (Blue)

Cementum covers the root under the gumline. Like enamel on the surface, cementum provides protection for the dentin in the root area.

The innermost part of the tooth is the **pulp.** It is made up of blood vessels which provide nourishment and nerve cells which transmit messages to the brain.

The **root** is the part of the tooth which is implanted in the gum.

The **root canal** is the channel in the center of the tooth which contains the pulp.

Tooth Decay and Gum Disease

Tooth decay and gum disease are always lurking in the shadows, waiting to strike. Foods left on the teeth for only a few minutes can begin the process of decay. Here's how it works.

Saliva coats teeth with an invisible film.

Foods causing decay, such as sugars and starches, are taken into the mouth and broken down by the action of saliva and by chewing.

Bacteria and bits of food stick to the saliva film, forming *plaque*. Plaque and the salts in saliva produce *calculus* (tartar). Calculus causes decay.

Bacteria living off sugars and starches produce a strong acid, which eats away at the enamel. The tooth now has no defense against decay.

KEEPING YOUR TEETH CLEAN AND HEALTHY

Preventive medicine is the best medicine. There are two important steps that you can take to keep decay and disease under control.

Stick to a regular system of dental hygiene.
Eat healthy foods and go easy on sugars and starches.

Flossing

Toothbrushes are not totally effective in cleaning teeth. Sometimes food gets wedged in between teeth and is difficult to reach. Before brushing, use dental floss.

Dental floss is sold waxed or unwaxed. Most dentists recommend unwaxed floss because wax can get lodged between your teeth the way food does.

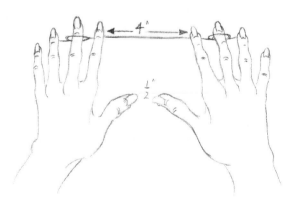

Pull out a length of floss about eighteen inches long. Holding the floss as indicated in the picture, slide it gently between your teeth in a back and forth motion. Do both sides of every tooth. Pay close attention to those back molars. Don't force it; it will snap.

Toothpaste

Toothpastes come in all shapes and colors. You can buy fluoride or non-fluoride; ammoniated or plain; paste, powder or gel; tube or pump; white, blue, green or striped.

Most dentists recommend fluoride toothpaste, since it helps prevent cavities. Fluoride bonds to the surface of the teeth to form a shield against decay. The water in some states contains natural fluoridation. In other areas, fluoride is added to the water. You can have fluoride applied directly to your teeth by your dentist or you can take it in vitamin form.

The important thing to remember about a toothpaste is that it is meant to clean your teeth with as little wear and tear on your enamel as possible.

> **TIP:** Toothpastes which promise to whiten and brighten your teeth are usually highly abrasive and acidic. That means they're hard on tooth enamel.

Brushing

Now you're ready for brushing. Choose a toothbrush with soft to medium round bristles. Over a period of time, hard bristles tend to wear down tooth enamel. Holding the brush parallel to the gumline, brush in an *up and down* motion. Study the following illustrations. Brush down from the upper teeth and up from the lower teeth.

> **TIP:** Enamel is thinnest at the gumline, so be especially careful there.

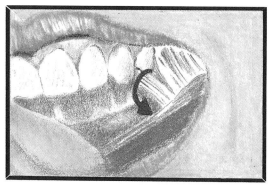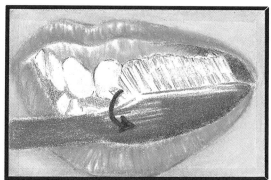

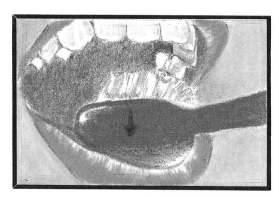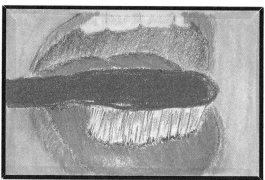

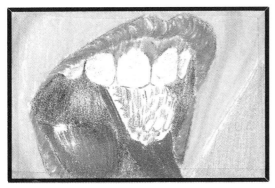
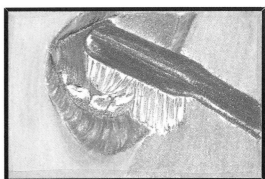
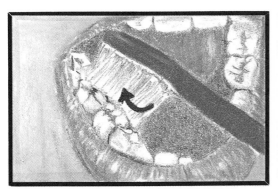
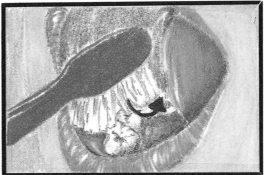

Precision and thoroughness are the name of the game here.
Remember the backs of the front teeth and the insides
of the molars. Make sure you reach all surfaces. While you're
at it, give your tongue a brush too.

Water Irrigators

Some people like to finish off their daily cleaning routine by using a **water irrigator**. Irrigators force water under pressure onto teeth and gums. Pressurized water has great force and can dislodge bits of food in hard to reach places. Like mouthwash, irrigators should not be used as a substitute for brushing. However, they are a useful tool.

There are a number of brands on the market. Follow the instructions carefully. Some irrigators come with containers that attach to the main unit. Some irrigators attach directly onto the faucet. Pressurized water is then forced out through a pick.

Irrigators are simple to use, once you get the hang of them. Direct the water to the base of each tooth, keeping the pressure set at low. You can increase the pressure gradually. Avoid high settings or you'll give your gums a blast they didn't expect.

TIP: Remember to put the pick in your mouth **before** you push the start button or you'll spray your bathroom!

Vitamins and Your Teeth

Vitamin A (Retinol) maintains healthy skin, bones, respiratory and digestive systems, helps ward off nose and throat infections. Vitamin A is found in eggs, milk, fish liver oils, green and yellow vegetables.

Vitamin B1 (Thiamine) is needed for metabolism and energy, keeps the nervous system and heart functioning properly. Vitamin B1 is found in whole grain breads, cereals, nuts, beans and meats.

Vitamin B2 (Riboflavin) enables the body to get energy from food and helps in body growth. Dairy products, green vegetables, cereals and whole grain breads contain Vitamin B2.

Vitamin B12 is needed for red blood cells, nerves, and aids in growth. Milk products, liver, and fish contain this vitamin.

Vitamin C (Ascorbic acid) is essential to the maintainance of healthy gums, teeth and bones. It protects against colds. Look for Vitamin C in citrus fruits, tomatoes, green vegetables, and potatoes.

Vitamin D builds bones and teeth by making use of the calcium and phosphorus in foods. Vitamin D can be found in liver, sardines, eggs, fish, and sunlight.

Vitamin K helps blood to clot. Vitamin K is found in all dark green leafy vegetables.

VISITING THE DENTIST

No matter how diligent you are about cleaning your teeth, bits of food always seem to get stuck somewhere. This is one reason why you should visit your dentist every six months. He or she will want to check the general health of your teeth and gums. A good dentist will watch the progress of your adult teeth. Should there be any problems, he can recommend a specialist to help you.

The first time you visit a dentist the receptionist will give you a questionnaire to fill out. The questions are simple and easy to answer.

> **TIP:** **It is very important that you fill this questionnaire out truthfully and completely.** Be especially careful when answering the medical questions. People with illnesses or allergies cannot tolerate some drugs or medical procedures. If you have health problems, be sure the dentist knows about them.

Before you actually see the dentist, you or your parent should ask the receptionist about the dentist's fees. A good time to do this is when you are returning the questionnaire to her desk. Dentists have set fees for each medical procedure.

The first thing the dentist will do is examine your entire mouth thoroughly. He'll check for cavities, gum disease and other abnormalities. If you're having problems with your mouth or teeth, now is the time to mention it.

Are your gums swollen or red?
Do they bleed when you brush your teeth?
Do you have a constant bad taste in your mouth?
Do you have halitosis (bad breath)?
Do you get sores in your mouth or on your lips?
Are you sensitive to hot or cold liquids?
Are any of your permanent teeth getting loose?

X-Rays

X-rays are useful tools. If you have a cavity lurking in a hard-to-see area, an X-ray can show it clearly. If some of your adult teeth have not come in yet, an X-ray can show how they are dropping even before they erupt from your gum.

There are two types of dental X-rays: pan X-rays, which take a single picture of your entire mouth, and tab X-rays, which show a small section of your mouth.

Some people still get anxious at the thought of having X-rays. That's because old fashioned X-ray equipment exposed the patient to a large dose of harmful radiation. With today's modern equipment, exposure is at a minimum.

> **TIP:** One full mouth X-ray is equivalent in radiation to standing in the sun on a beach for ten minutes.

There is no need to be overly macho about this, however. Ask the dentist for a lead apron. This will cover your body from the neck down. Lead stops radiation from entering anything it covers.

Cleaning Your Teeth

If you're feeling well and the dentist can't find anything wrong, he will probably recommend a good cleaning. Basically, a cleaning involves three procedures.

Scaling is necessary to remove all the hardened calculus that's hiding under your gumline. There's going to be some bleeding and some pain. Hang on; everybody goes through this. You can too. Nobody is deliberately trying to make you uncomfortable. This procedure cannot be skipped if you want to get your teeth really clean and keep healthy gums.

Now you're ready for **polishing**. The dentist will polish your teeth with baking soda. Dentists used to use pumice, but pumice wears down the enamel. Baking soda is a mild abrasive which smooths over the rough edges on your teeth. You want your teeth to be smooth because cavities love to grow in pits and rough spots.

After your teeth are clean and gorgeous again, the dentist may do some **flossing**. This is the same procedure we talked about earlier. Flossing removes the remaining abrasive from between the teeth.

Filling a Cavity

Since we get far too many cavities, fillings are a common dental procedure. If you've never had a cavity filled, you'll probably feel better if you know what to expect.

The dentist will take an X-ray to determine exactly where the cavity is. Next he will give you an *anesthetic* (pain killer). Now the dentist must remove all the decay from your tooth. This is an important step because, if the decay is not removed, it will spread. Don't panic when you see that drill coming at you. The anesthetic has deadened your nerve endings and you won't feel anything. With the decay removed, the dentist will place filler in the hole and mold it into the shape of the original tooth.

Dentists can choose from among a number of filler materials. *Silver amalgam* is the most popular because it is easy to use and hardens quickly. *Gold* is expensive, but it is very strong and durable. It is used for extensive work on the back teeth. *White composite materials* can be made to match the color of the tooth exactly. When the filling has hardened into shape you're finished! That wasn't so bad.

> **TIP:** Don't try to eat or drink until all of the anesthetic has worn off or until you have regained control of your muscles. Without muscle control you might choke or bite your tongue.

In order to avoid the need for future fillings, you'll want to keep your teeth and gums really clean. To see how well you are cleaning between office visits, ask your dentist for some *disclosing tablets*. He will tell you how to use them. Usually you chew one or two tablets and swish the liquid around your mouth for about half a minute. Now look in the mirror. All the discolored spots are places where you have plaque.

COOKS CORNER INTERMEDIATE
MEDIA CENTER

BRACES AND YOU

Occlusion and Malocclusion

When the teeth of the upper jaw mesh with the teeth of the lower jaw, the process is called **occlusion**. If done correctly, this involves 128 contact points.

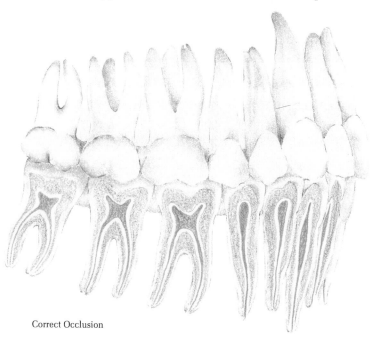

Correct Occlusion

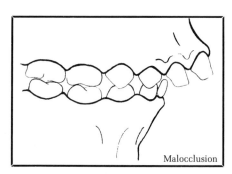

Malocclusion

Malocclusion is also known as "bad bite." It means that the teeth do not fit together properly and the bite is not correct.

What causes bad bite?

Genetics, you were born with it.

You started out with good bite when you had your baby teeth but, when they dropped out, the adult teeth did not follow the proper eruption pattern. Perhaps your teeth and jaws were not properly positioned causing the permanent teeth to come in out of line.

Some people have jaws which are just too small to accommodate the size and number of permanent teeth.

Bad habits, such as thumb sucking, can put undue pressure on erupting teeth causing them to come in at strange angles.

What happens if you don't correct bad bite?

Not only does malocclusion spoil your looks, but it can lead to some serious dental problems.

Pressure is put on surrounding teeth causing them to loosen. You may even lose good teeth.

Ear canal problems can develop.

Poor alignment (improper spacing) makes it more difficult for you to brush your teeth properly. Food can get trapped in hard-to-get-at areas resulting in tooth decay.

Some teeth may become *impacted*. That means that the crowding of surrounding teeth prevents the tooth from growing in straight.

Headaches may be a symptom of dental problems.

Seeing An Orthodontist

So many people have crooked teeth that going to an orthodontist seems to be one of the natural steps in growing up. Orthodontists are dentists who straighten teeth with the use of braces and other appliances.

The orthodontist will examine your mouth carefully to see if you really do need braces. If you do, he or she will take a case history, an X-ray and an **impression** of your mouth. This is done by covering all your teeth with a jelly-like substance and leaving it on for a few minutes until it hardens. With this impression your orthodontist will be able to see the positioning of every tooth in your mouth. This impression is called a **mold**, and it is used to cast models of your teeth. Ask to see your mold. It's interesting to look at your teeth from outside your body.

Generally, orthodontists use **braces** to align teeth. Braces are made of metal or a transparent material and fit on your teeth. The teeth are pressured into correct alignment by the tightening or loosening of the wires which attach to the braces. While your braces are on, you need to see your orthodontist regularly because he will want to adjust the wires as your teeth move. You may feel some discomfort right after the wires are tightened. This is normal. If the discomfort persists, ask your orthodontist about it.

If he wants to push the back molars further back to make room in the front of your mouth, he might use an **arch wire**. The wire is attached to a brace which is fitted around the tooth to be moved. The wire goes across the front of the mouth and is attached to a strap, which goes behind the neck. The tension between the front wire and the back strap keeps the appliance in place.

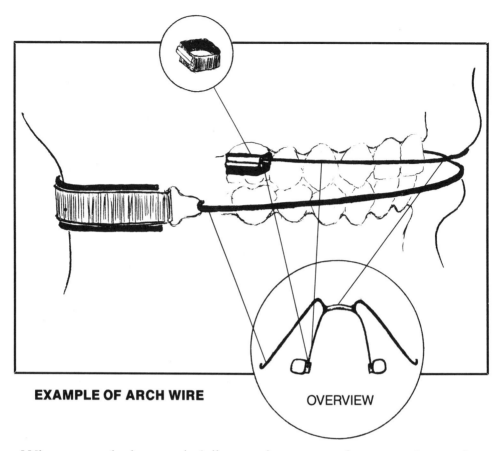

EXAMPLE OF ARCH WIRE

OVERVIEW

When your baby teeth fall out, the space that remains waits for the adult tooth still in the jaw to make its appearance. It is important that the space be reserved for this incoming tooth only. If you orthodontist sees a side tooth trying to cut into this territory, he may put in a **space maintainer**. A space maintainer holds the space open for the erupting tooth, while keeping its neighbors at bay.

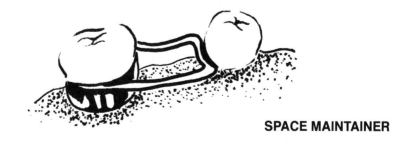

SPACE MAINTAINER

General Rules for Living with Braces

It is vitally important that you keep up a consistent program of good dental hygiene. Food deposits left under braces are very difficult to detect. When your braces are removed, you don't want to find that you have a mouth full of cavities.

Avoid chewing gum while your braces are in. Gum is almost impossible to remove.

You may find that your speech is temporarily affected.

Don't make any adjustment on an appliance by yourself! You could be doing more harm than good.

If you're experiencing an unusual amount of discomfort, call your orthodontist.

Lighten up on the sugars and starches; they promote decay.

If something breaks, don't try to fix it yourself. Call the orthodontist.

If you have a removable appliance, be sure to keep it in a safe, clean place where it won't be bothered by brothers, sisters or pets.

Make sure your appliance is clean before you put it in your mouth.

If you have a removable appliance, be grown-up enough to wear it. Cheating will only prolong the time you have to wear braces.

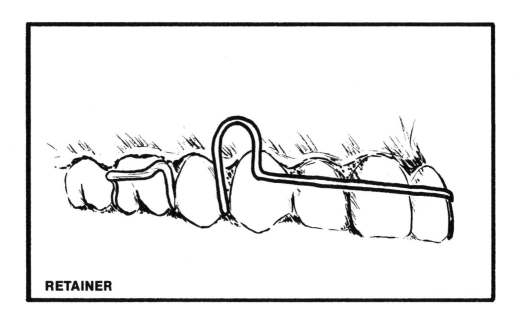

RETAINER

When your braces are removed, the orthodontist may give you a **retainer**. Retainers keep the teeth in their correct new positions while the jawbone hardens. Wear your retainer or your teeth may return to their old positions.

Cooperate with your orthodontist.

TIP: It may be possible to avoid the "tinsel teeth" look. Ask your orthodontist about **lingual appliances**. They are brackets which attach to the backs of your teeth and are invisible from the front. Remember to discuss cost. Lingual braces are more expensive than metal braces.

PROBLEMS THAT CAN ARISE

Pain is a signal from your body that something is wrong. Problems do not go away by themselves. Listen to what your body is trying to tell you.

Some people who are nervous and under a lot of pressure grind their teeth and clench their jaws. They may do this so fiercely that they actually develop headaches and aching jaws. This practice is called **bruxism**. If you find yourself grinding your teeth, try to relax. Ask your dentist for a *night guard* to keep you from grinding in your sleep.

A **canker sore** is a small ulcer in the lining of the mouth. It can be caused by a virus, pressure from a tooth, or a nervous habit of biting your tongue or cheek. Certain foods high in acid, such as vinegar, wine and citrus juices, may cause canker sores. They may also occur just before menstruation. Your dentist can recommend a colorless gel to clear up this condition.

> **TIP:** Some people believe that you can cure a sore or stop a toothache by chewing on aspirin. **NEVER** chew aspirin. Aspirin is a strong acid that burns tissue.

Sometimes bad habits can cause mouth problems. Cigarettes and chewing tobacco stain your teeth and leave you with an anti-social case of bad breath. Juices from chewing tobacco can damage delicate mouth tissue, causing it to become white and leathery-looking. This condition is called **leukoplakia** and can lead to oral cancer.

Periodontal diseases affect the gums. They occur when the build-up of plaque around the teeth is so great that the gums become inflamed. There are three main periodontal diseases.

Trench mouth (Vincent's Infection) occurs when the body is in a rundown condition due to inadequate nutrition and poor dental habits. Bacteria in the mouth cause bleeding gums, ulcers, sore throat, fever, swollen glands and severe bad breath. If nothing is done about trench mouth it can lead to more serious diseases like gingivitis and periodontitis. If you suspect you have trench mouth, see a dentist immediately, and begin a diet with lots of fresh fruit and vegetables and plenty of water.

Gingivitis is a gum disease characterized by red swollen gums, which bleed easily when brushed. Your dentist will remove all plaque from the gums and, no doubt, tell you to do a better job of brushing.

Periodontitis can develop from untreated gingivitis. This is a serious infection which destroys the walls around the teeth. The gums recede and ooze a yellowish pus. The teeth become loose and fall out.

Emergency Procedures

Toothache — rinse out the mouth with warm water. Try flossing, since there may be a piece of food between your teeth which is causing the trouble. If the ache persists, see your dentist.

Fractured Jaw — avoid moving the jaw. Go to a dentist or an emergency room. Apply cold compresses.

Broken Tooth — clean any dirt around the area using warm water. Cold compresses will reduce the swelling. Save the tooth and bring it with you to the dentist. He may be able to bond it to the broken fragment.

Bitten Tongue or Lip — use a clean cloth to apply pressure to the area. Pressure stops bleeding. Reduce swelling with cold compresses. If you can't stop the bleeding, go to a dentist or a hospital emergency room.

Dentists and Their Specialties

A **dentist** is a medical doctor who is concerned with the well being of the entire mouth.

The word "pediatric" has to do with the care of children. A **pediatric dentist** is a dentist who treats children and adolescents.

An **orthodontist** uses braces and other corrective appliances to straighten crooked teeth and improve bite.

Gum disease (gingivitis) is treated by a **periodontist**.

Surgery on the entire mouth area and tooth extraction is done by an **oral surgeon**.

Problems that affect the pulp of the tooth are treated by an **endodontist**.

A **dental hygienist** is not a medical doctor. He or she specializes in the cleaning of the teeth. In a busy office, the dentist may not have time to clean teeth. The hygienist will do it.

BIBLIOGRAPHY

"Great Teeth," Vogue Magazine, March 1987, p. 212.

Good Mouthkeeping: or How to Save Your Children's Teeth and Your Own While You're At It, John Besford. Oxford University Press, 1984.

Nutrition and Dental Health, Ann Ehrlich. Delmar, 1987.

The Story of How Judy Saved Her Teeth: Nutrition Made Easy, Catherine J. Frompovich. Frompovich, 1982.

"Health Style—Drill-free Dentistry," Vogue Magazine, June 1987, p. 264.

The Tooth Trip, Thomas McGuire. Random, 1972.

How to Save Your Teeth, Howard B. Marshall. Penguin, 1982.

"Health Style—Tooth-Prepping," Vogue Magazine, March 1987, p. 520.

A Prevention-Oriented School Based Dental Program, American Dental Association.

Tooth Survival Book, American Dental Association.

How to Cope with Braces, Jeanne Betancourt. Knopf, 1982.

Teeth, John Gaskin (Your Body Series). Watts, 1984.

Bleaching Teeth, Feinman and Goldstein. Quint Publishing Company, 1987.

The Complete Family Guide to Dental Health, Jacob Himler. McGraw-Hill, 1978.

Learning About Your Oral Health, American Dental Association.

INDEX

Alignment, 21, 23
Anesthetic, 19
Arch wire, 23
Aspirin, 27

Bacteria, 9, 28
Bad bite
   (see malocclusion), 20
Bicuspids, 7
Blood vessels, 9
Braces, 20, 23
Brushing, 11, 12, 13
Bruxism, 27

Calculus, 9
Canine, 4, 6, 7
Canker sore, 27
Cavities, 17, 18
Cementum, 8, 9
Crown, 7, 8
Cusps, 7, 8

Deciduous, 4, 6
Dental hygienist, 29
Dentin, 7, 8
Disclosing tablets, 19

Ear canal, 21
Enamel, 7, 8, 11
Endodontist, 29

Flossing, 10, 18
Fluoride, 11
Fractured jaw, 28

Gingivitis, 28
Gold, 19
Gum disease, 28
Gums, 8, 9, 18

Halitosis, 17, 27, 28
Headaches, 21, 27

Impacted, 21
Impression, 23
Incisor, 4, 6, 7

Jaw, 4, 21

Lead apron, 17
Leukoplakia, 27
Lingual appliances, 26

Malocclusion, 20, 21
Molar, 4, 6, 7, 8, 13, 23
Mold, 23

Nerve cells, 8
Night guard, 27

Occlusion, 20

INDEX (continued)

Oral cancer, 27
Oral surgeon, 29
Orthodontist, 23, 29

Pediatric dentist, 29
Periodontal diseases, 28
Periodontist, 29
Periodontitis, 28
Permanent, 4, 6, 21
Plaque, 9, 28
Polishing, 18
Premolar, 4, 6, 7
Pulp, 8, 9

Questionnaire, 16

Radiation, 17
Retainer, 26
Root canal, 9
Roots, 8, 9

Saliva, 4, 9
Scaling, 18
Sensitivity to cold/hot, 17
Silver amalgam, 19
Sores, 17
Space maintainer, 24
Starch, 9, 10, 25
Sugar, 9, 10, 25

Tartar, 9
Thumb sucking, 21
Tongue, 4, 13, 29
Tooth decay, 9
Toothache, 28
Toothpaste, 11
Trench mouth, 28

Vitamins, 15

Water irrigators, 14
White composite
    materials, 19
Wisdom teeth, 7

X-Rays, 17, 19, 23